P9-BBV-770

The Grandmother Book

A Book About You for Your Grandchild

The Grandmother Book

A Book About You for Your Grandchild

Andy and Susan Hilford

Andrews McMeel Publishing, LLC
Kansas City

To Tessa and Tyler's Grandparents

With Love

For sharing the stories and wisdom of their journey and paving the road for the future

The Grandmother Book

Copyright © 2008 by Andy and Susan Hilford. All rights reserved. Printed in China. No part of this book may be used or reproduced in any manner whatsoever without written permission except in the case of reprints in the context of reviews. For information, write Andrews McMeel Publishing, LLC, an Andrews McMeel Universal company, 1130 Walnut Street, Kansas City, MO 64106.

09 10 11 12 TEN 10 9 8 7 6 5 4 3

ISBN-13: 978-0-7407-7112-5
ISBN-10: 0-7407-7112-4

www.andrewsmcmeel.com

Illustrations by David Walker
Book design by Diane Marsh

ATTENTION: SCHOOLS AND BUSINESSES
Andrews McMeel books are available at quantity discounts with bulk purchase for educational, business, or sales promotional use. For information, please write to: Special Sales Department, Andrews McMeel Publishing, LLC, 1130 Walnut Street, Kansas City, Mo 64106.

This is the other baby book. It's not about your grandchild, it's about you—but it's *for* your grandchild. In the coming pages are places for you to put together the story of you—the thoughts, moments, events, images, ideas, and, yup, even some of those "What was I thinking?" moments, ones that add, um, *depth* to your story. These answers and pictures are the tiles of your autobiographical mosaic—the narrative of the "you" that came before your grandchild arrived on the scene.

In the pages of this book you'll find lots of questions along with a number of places to put particular pictures. Writing your story can take a few days or months or years to complete—whatever works for you. The questions and picture themes were selected to give your grandchild a ____________________ (fill in the blank) book about you. And, of course, remember, this is not an essay test with required responses. You don't have to answer everything. You don't have to answer any question as it's written. If any questions don't apply to you, skip them, cross them out, or change them entirely. If you want to put in something that doesn't appear in any of the pages, great, add it. It's your story to tell.

Sometime down the road, your grandchild will sit him- or herself down in a comfortable chair and have quite the read.

Enjoy.

fun! smiles you

true love Grandparen

first hom

Big Day

family tree

so happy adventure

memories school

very first time Life

friends Celebrations

honeymoon Wow

Here's lookin' at you, kid

This book is for you . . .

Here goes . . .

Grandmother's full name is . . . .

I was born in (year and location) . . . .

. . . .

In that year (what historical things happened) . . . .

. . . .

. . . .

. . . .

I weighed . . . .

I looked just like . . . .

. . . .

As a baby I was a *horrible* *average* *good* *couldn't be stopped* eater.

I was one of (number) . . . . children.

My siblings' names are . . . .

. . . .

. . . .

Our family didn't always live in the United States.

Here's how we ended up here:

. . . .

. . . .

. . . .

. . . .

. . . .

. . . .

More Thoughts . . . .

. . . .

. . . .

. . . .

. . . .

. . . .

Oooo, look at those cheeks!

Picture(s) of Young Grandmother

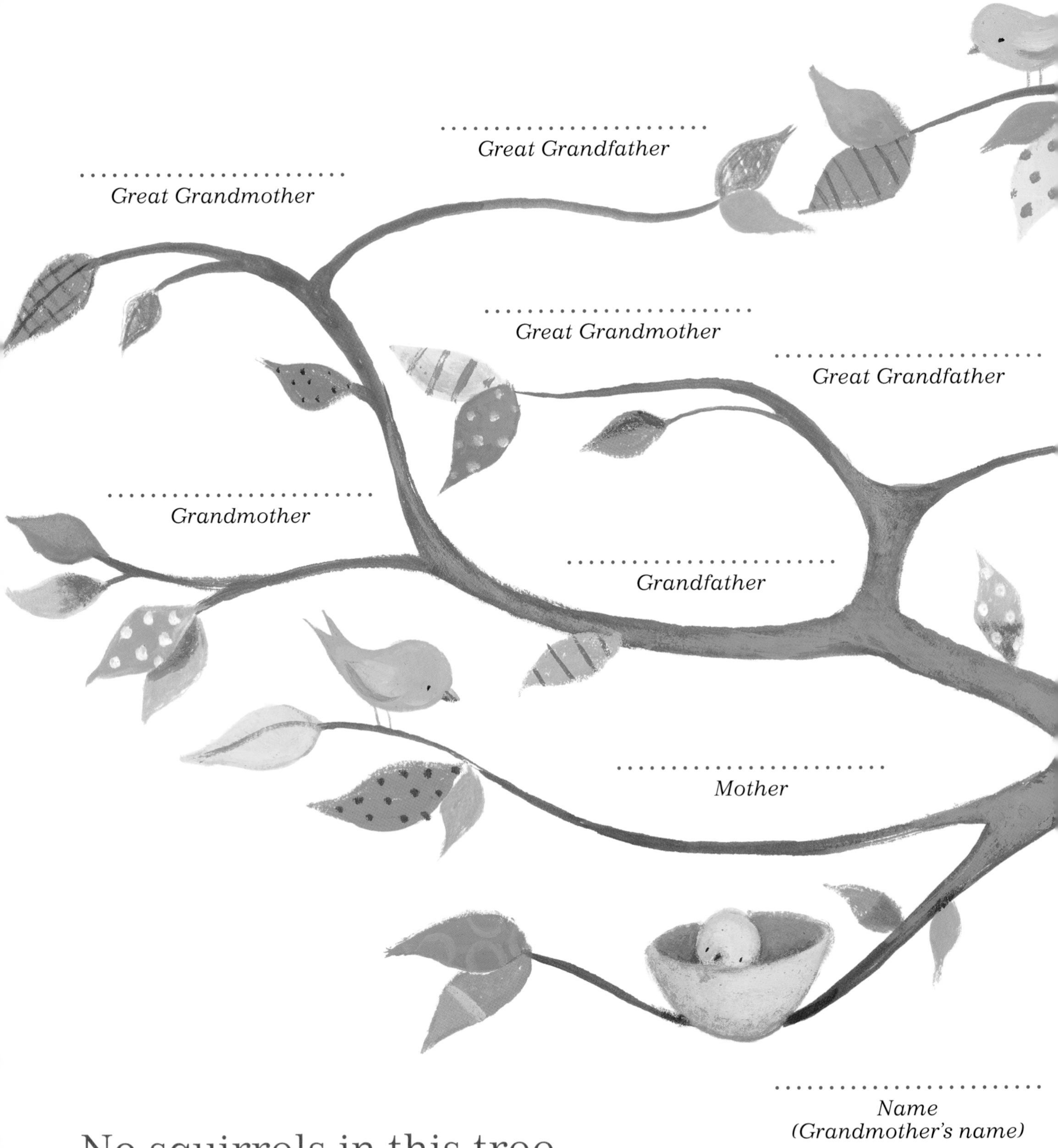

No squirrels in this tree (but maybe a few nuts)

Grandmother's Family Tree

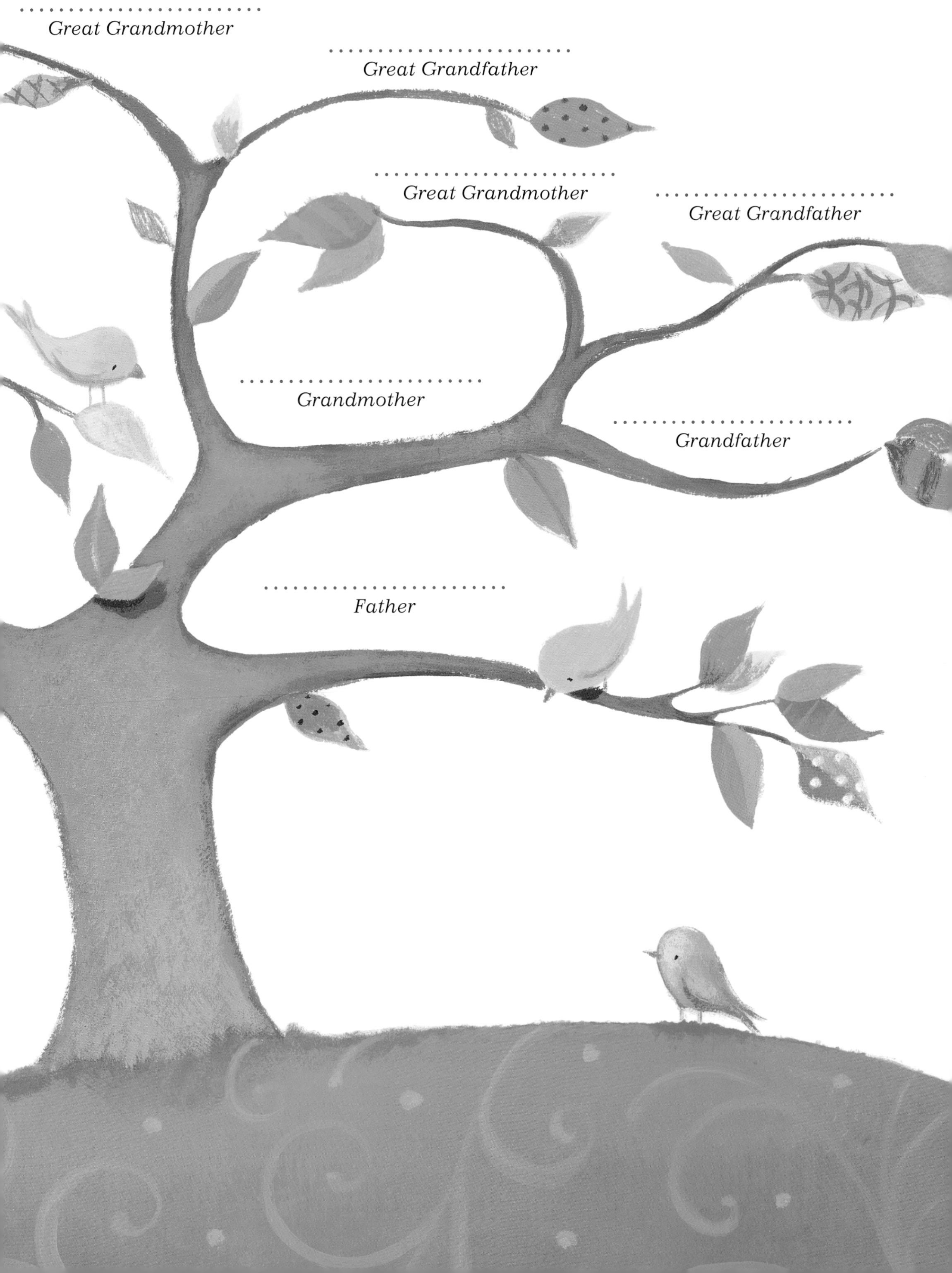
Great Grandmother
Great Grandfather
Great Grandmother
Great Grandfather
Grandmother
Grandfather
Father

When I was young (waaaay back when)

I grew up in ...

The address was ...

We lived in (what kind of home) ...

The family car was ...

New, the car probably cost ...

When I was little, I got an allowance of ...

My favorite treat was ...

For Halloween, my favorite costume was ...

Our family pet was ...

For family vacation, we once went to ...

I remember listening to (on the radio) ...

The first movie I remember seeing was ...

In grade school, my bedtime was ...

When I thought about being an adult, I thought ...

I went to grade school at

The school was (how big: how many students/classes)

My favorite subjects were

I was probably a (what kind of pupil)

I once got in trouble for

I liked (playing/doing)

I did (sports/clubs/instruments)

More Thoughts

Sugar and Spice and Everything Nice

Picture(s) of Grandmother in Grade School

Postadolescence wasn't any easier back then

I started high school in (year) ....

and .... was president.

I went to high school at ....

I liked doing ....

....

My best friends were (names) ....

....

My favorite subjects were ....

....

My teachers would probably describe me as ....

....

I did (clubs/sports/musical instruments) ....

....

I remember listening to (on the radio) ....

....

After school, I worked at (where) ....

and made about (how much an hour) ....

A hamburger, fries, and a soda cost about ....

My first date was (when/where/who) ....

....

....

When I got dressed up, I wore ....

....

A movie cost ....

On a regular Friday or Saturday night, I probably (did what) ....

....

....

I once got "grounded" for ....

....

I remember reading (which books/magazines) ....

....

When I was in high school, the really popular songs were

(songs and bands) ....

....

The biggest actors were (names) ....

....

My senior prom was ....

....

....

When I thought about the twenty-first century, I probably thought it

....

....

....

More Thoughts ....

....

....

....

....

....

You went out in public like that?

Picture(s) of Grandmother in High School

High School Report Card

Leaving the nest
(about as fast as my feet would take me)

I went to college (where and when)

In that year (what historical things happened)

Tuition cost about

I majored in

One of my favorite classes was

The best professor I had was ,

because

The worst class I had was ,

because

I liked doing

I belonged to (sorority, clubs, teams)

My friends probably described me as

Check one: I spent a lot of time at the library . . . . ;

I went to the library only when I had to . . . . ;

there was a library? . . . .

On a weekend night I usually . . . .

. . . .

. . . .

I definitely *did* *did not* know all the words to my college song

(We had a school song?) . . . .

. . . .

. . . .

My biggest accomplishments in college were . . . .

. . . .

. . . .

More Thoughts . . . .

. . . .

. . . .

. . . .

. . . .

. . . .

Footloose and fancy free!

Picture(s) of Grandmother in College

Grandmother goes wild(ish) . . .

During the summers, I . . . .

. . . .

On a typical weekend night in the summer, I . . . .

. . . .

. . . .

The best part of summer was . . . .

. . . .

It was during the summer of (what year) . . . . that I

(did what) . . . .

. . . .

The nuttiest thing I did during summer vacation was . . . .

. . . .

The most interesting place I remember visiting during summer was

. . . .

I liked it because . . . .

. . . .

The memory that sticks out most from those summers is . . . .

. . . .

I can't believe I'm writing this, but once I . . . .

. . . .

More Thoughts

Don’t ever show these to your parents!

(Promise?)

Picture(s) of Grandmother on Vacation from College

Yikes! Work . . .

My first full-time job was ....

....

The first company I worked for was ....

I stayed with the company for (how long) ....

....

My title was ....

My salary was ....

My responsibilities included ....

....

It would be (how long) .... before I used a computer.

I wore (what was the dress code) ....

.... to work

My boss ....

The best part of my job was ....

....

The worst part of my job was ....

....

The thing that I now most remember about that job is ....

....

More Thoughts

Grandmother's hall of fame

My favorite movies of all time are ....

....

My favorite television shows of all time are ....

....

My favorite bands/songs/lyrics of all time are ....

....

My favorite places in the world are ....

....

My favorite books of all time are ....

....

My favorite actors ever are ....

....

My favorite foods of all time are ....

....

If you ever have the chance, you should ....

....

My biggest accomplishments ever are ....

....

My favorite vacation was ....

....

The most exciting vacation I ever took was ....

....

The most romantic trip I ever took was . . . .

. . . .

During my lifetime, the most interesting historical moments were

. . . .

. . . .

When I could do whatever I wanted, my favorite things to do were

. . . .

. . . .

I think the people who did most to change the world are . . . .

. . . .

. . . .

I think the inventions that did most to change the world are . . . .

. . . .

. . . .

More Thoughts . . . .

. . . .

. . . .

. . . .

. . . .

. . . .

. . . .

My knight in shining armor

The first time I met your grandfather, I was *single* *looking* *dating*

and .... years old.

We *met at a party* *were set up* *worked together* ....

The first time I saw him I thought ....

....

On our first date we went to ....

On a scale of one to ten, I would rate the date ....

About seeing him again, I thought ....

We kissed on the .... date

He used to *always* *sometimes* *barely ever* *are you kidding?*

write me love letters.

My parents thought he was ....

....

....

One of the most memorable dates we went on was

....

One of the most unusual dates we went on was

....

Our most romantic Valentine's Day was

....

More Thoughts

Oh, this is it! This is it!

I knew he was the one when

My friends all thought

He proposed to me on (day/month/year)

I remember the day being

My first thought when he started to propose was

It took me (how long) to say "yes"

The ring was

That night, we celebrated by

The first people I told were . . . .

. . . .

. . . .

Their reaction was . . . .

. . . .

. . . .

Here's how your grandfather proposed. It was . . . .

. . . .

. . . .

. . . .

. . . .

More Thoughts

. . . .

. . . .

. . . .

. . . .

. . . .

. . . .

We danced the night away

We got married on (date) . . . .

at (where) . . . .

. . . .

My wedding dress was . . . .

. . . .

My maid of honor was (name) . . . .

She wore . . . .

We had (number) . . . . guests

We were married by . . . .

Just before the ceremony started, I was thinking . . . .

. . . .

I was absolutely the most nervous during . . . .

. . . .

During the ceremony . . . .

. . . .

For music we had . . . .

Our first song was . . . .

The best wedding present we received was . . . .

. . . .

The weirdest wedding present we received was . . . .

. . . .

The one thing that stands out in my memory about the wedding is

. . . .

. . . .

The most awkward moment of that day was . . . .

. . . .

We spent our first night as a married couple at . . . .

. . . .

My fondest memory of that day is . . . .

. . . .

. . . .

More Thoughts . . . .

. . . .

. . . .

. . . .

. . . .

. . . .

All aboard . . .

For our honeymoon, we went to ....

....

Our honeymoon lasted (number) .... days.

We stayed at (hotels/places) ....

....

What I thought about being called Mrs. (..........) ....

....

My favorite place on the trip was ....

....

Our typical day was *busy* *relaxed* *we never really were awake during the day*

We (did what activities) ....

....

One of the best moments of the honeymoon was ....

....

One of the oddest moments of the honeymoon was ....

....

One thing that stands out when I think about the honeymoon is ......

....

More Thoughts ....

....

....

....

....

....

Mmmmmmm, honeymoon

Picture(s) of the Honeymoon

Grandfather Studmuffin

The thing I love most about Grandfather is . . . .

. . . .

. . . .

My favorite thing about Grandfather's personality is . . . .

. . . .

. . . .

His cutest feature is . . . .

. . . .

The thing that impressed me most about him is . . . .

. . . .

My parents thought he . . . .

. . . .

To make me laugh, he . . . .

. . . .

The one meal I made that was Grandfather's absolute favorite was

. . . .

. . . .

He once surprised me by . . . .

. . . .

. . . .

The most romantic thing he ever did . . . .

. . . .

. . . .

My nickname(s) for him is . . . .

I thought he looked most handsome when he wore . . . .

. . . .

. . . .

More Thoughts . . . .

. . . .

. . . .

. . . .

. . . .

. . . .

Home Sweet Home

Our first home was at (address) ....

....

The house was a ....

....

It cost ....

The neighborhood was ....

....

I thought Grandfather's stuff was ....

....

We bought our first car (when) ....

It was a ....

It cost ....

My favorite part of the house was ....,

because ....

....

On a typical night, we would ....

....

For our first anniversary, we ....

....

Our first big purchase together was ....

....

More Thoughts ....

....

....

....

....

....

....

Well, see, back then we . . .

In the old days, phones . . . .

. . . .

The lowest price I can remember paying for a can of soda was . . . .

. . . .

Babysitting cost about (how much) . . . . an hour.

My favorite game as a child was . . . .

. . . .

When the first man landed on the moon, I was . . . .

. . . .

A good salary was about . . . .

. . . .

The first car I learned to drive was . . . .

. . . .

The first time I flew, I was . . . .

. . . .

I went from . . . . to . . . .

It cost about . . . .

The first computer I ever used was ....

....

The most famous person I ever met was ....

....

....

It may be common today, but as a teenager I never would have believed

that every house would have a ....

....

....

More Thoughts ....

....

....

....

....

....

....

When your parents told me that they were going to get married, I thought

When your parents told me that they were pregnant with you, I thought

More Thoughts

Sooooo cute!

Favorite Picture(s) of Grandmother and Child

Finally, a grandchild!

When you were born, I was . . . .

. . . .

The first thing I remember doing after I heard the news was . . . .

. . . .

The first time I saw you, I . . . .

. . . .

I thought you looked like . . . .

. . . .

The first time I held you . . . .

. . . .

My first impression of you was . . . .

. . . .

. . . .

. . . .

We played

One of my favorite things about you is

A characteristic we share in common is

The best thing about being a grandmother is

More Thoughts

Whoooweee, I'm going to spoil you silly

Picture(s) of Grandmother and Grandchild

Oh, and . . .

A Few More Thoughts from a Very Proud Grandmother